One Small Place in a Tree

By Barbara Brenner

Illustrated by Tom Leonard

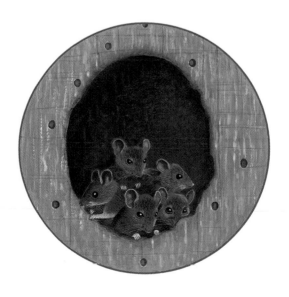

HarperCollins Publishers

To Rich Evans
and the HFCA Environmental Committee—B.B.

For my mother, who taught me what art is—T.L.

The author and illustrator would like to thank Dr. Thomas C. Harrington
from the Department of Plant Pathology at Iowa State University
for his contributions to this book.

One Small Place in a Tree · Text copyright © 2004 by Barbara Brenner · Illustrations copyright © 2004 by Tom Leonard
Manufactured in China by South China Printing Company Ltd.
All rights reserved. · www.harperchildrens.com · Library of Congress Cataloging-in-Publication Data · Brenner, Barbara.
One small place in a tree / by Barbara Brenner ; illustrated by Tom Leonard.—1st ed. · p.   cm.
Summary: A child visitor observes as one tiny scratch in a tree develops into a home for a variety of woodland animals
over many years, even after the tree has fallen.
ISBN 0-688-17180-X—ISBN 0-688-17181-8 (lib. bdg.)
1. Forest ecology—Juvenile literature. 2. Forest animals—Habitat—Juvenile literature. 3. Trees—Ecology—Juvenile literature.
[1. Forest Ecology. 2. Forest Animals. 3. Trees—Ecology. 4. Ecology.] I. Leonard, Tom, ill. II. Title.
QH541.5.F6 B69 2004   577.3—dc21   2002001181   CIP   AC
Designed by Stephanie Bart-Horvath · 6 7 8 9 10 · ❖ · First Edition

A tree hole.
One small place in a tree.
How does it get there?
Who lives inside?

Suppose that you could watch
a hole from its beginning.
You might see something like this:

Here's one oak tree in a forest.
It looks like the others, except—
a black bear uses this one
as a scratching post.
Every time she goes by,
the bear sharpens her claws
on the trunk.

You're walking in the woods.
You see the tree and notice
the scratch marks on the bark.
Maybe you even catch a glimpse
of the bear!

After a while the scratching chips
some pieces of bark off the tree.
A cut forms in the bark.
A hole in the tree is beginning.

Next time you're walking there, you
see that tiny bugs have found the cut.
They're timber beetles, and they're
about to set up housekeeping.

The timber beetles get under the bark
and bore into the tree.
They make a maze of tunnels.
They create spaces called cradles
for their eggs.
And they "plant" fungi for the colony
to feed on.
Imagine that you can look inside.
You see something like this.

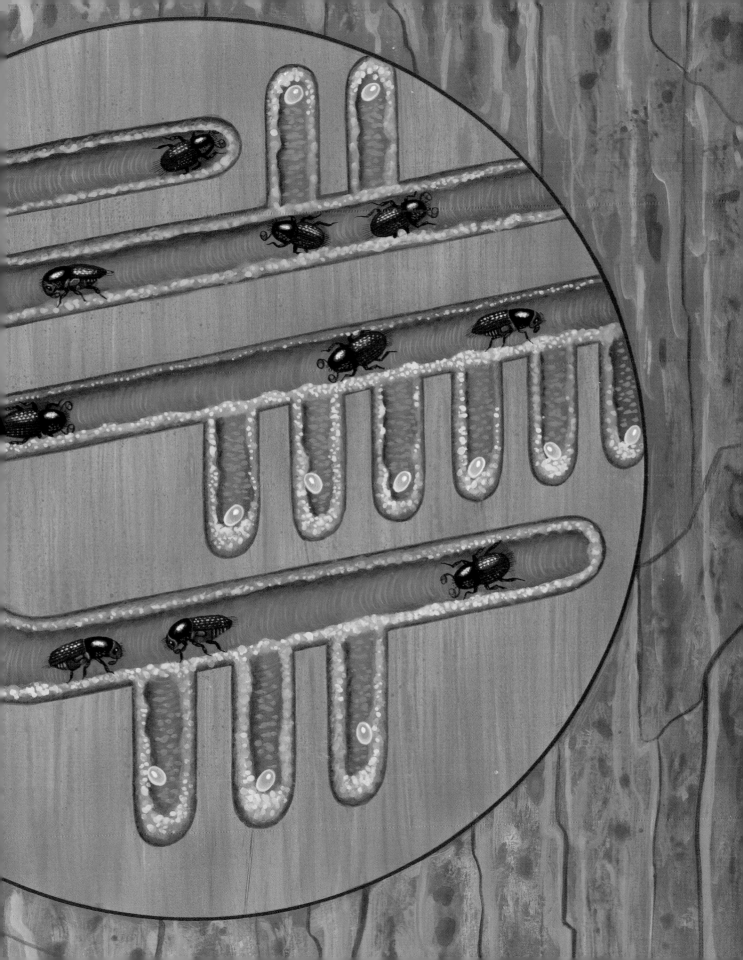

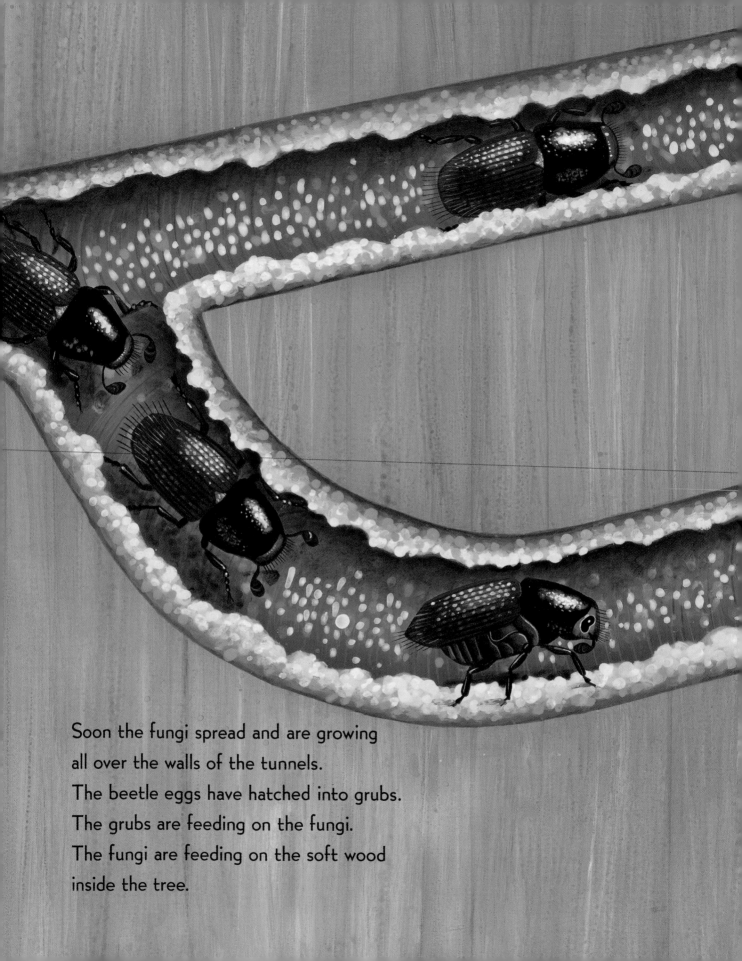

Soon the fungi spread and are growing
all over the walls of the tunnels.
The beetle eggs have hatched into grubs.
The grubs are feeding on the fungi.
The fungi are feeding on the soft wood
inside the tree.

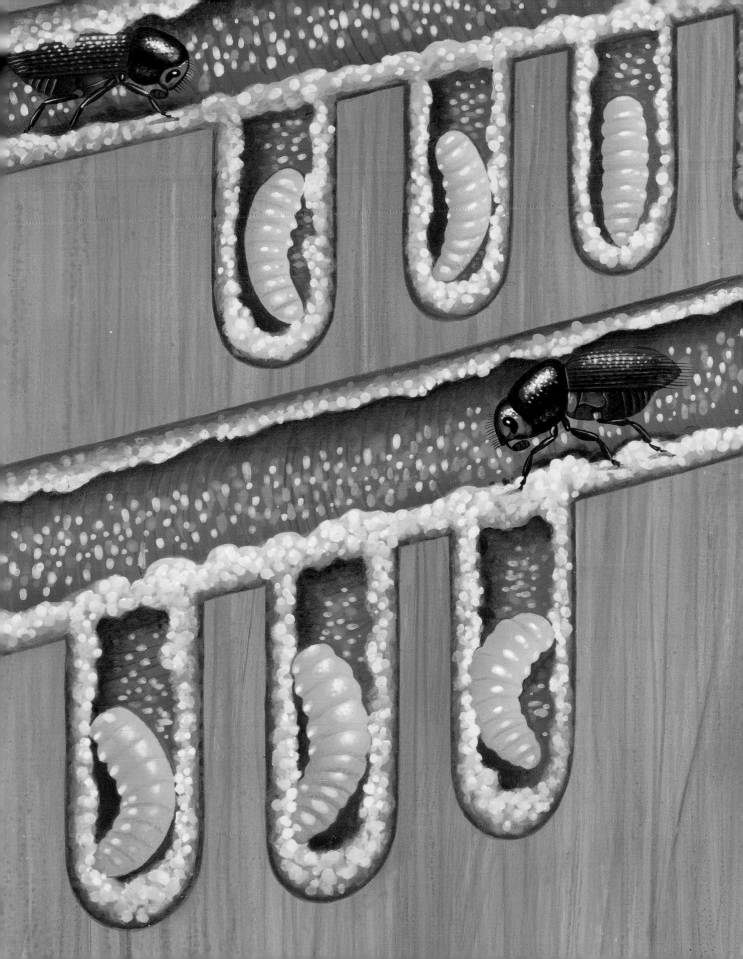

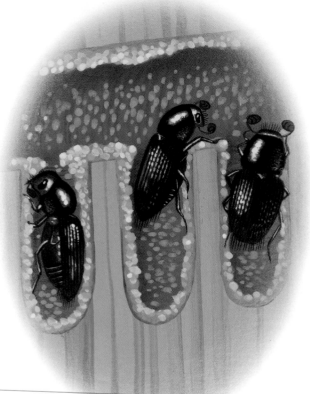

The beetle grubs become
full-grown timber beetles.

They eat their way out of the chambers
and make more holes in the tree.

On your next visit you count more than ten holes.
But the first one is the largest.

One time when you're near the tree, you actually hear the sound of the beetles chewing wood.

A red-bellied woodpecker hears it, too.

The bird flies to the tree holes. It spears the beetles with its sharp beak, or pulls them out with its long tongue.

Many woodpeckers visit the oak tree to eat. After a summer they've cleared the holes of beetles and beetle grubs. But they've made the big hole even bigger.

Now disease strikes.
Bacteria come in
through the hole in the tree.
You won't see the bacteria—
they're too small.
But you can see
the damage they've done.
The tree has heart rot.
It's dying inside and out.

Bark begins to loosen and fall off.
The hole is now so large
that you can actually see inside.

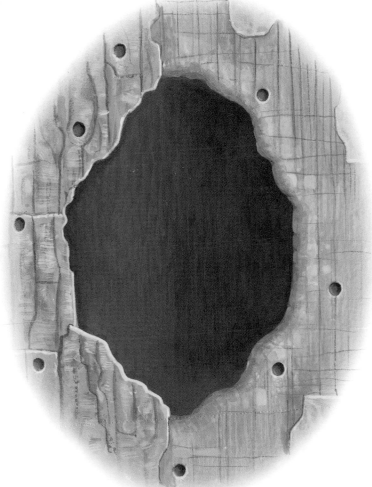

It has become a hollow place
that looks as if it could be
home for something.

The first animal to use it
is a flying squirrel.
You find the squirrel "holed up"
in there one winter day.
You notice that it has stored
some nuts under the loose bark
around the hole.

When you come by in the spring, the flying squirrel is gone.
The hole is empty, but not for long. A pair of bluebirds moves in.
The hole is just right for bluebirds—high enough off the ground for safety.

The bluebirds line the hole
with weeds and grass.
Soon there are six bluish eggs
in the nest hole.

Next time you look inside,
there are six bluebird chicks.
The chicks stay safe in the nest
until they're old enough to fly.

By this time the oak tree
is no longer sending out leaves.
Almost all of its bark is gone.
But the hole-dwellers don't
seem to care.

For the next three springs,
the hole in the tree is a nest
for the same pair of bluebirds.

For the next three winters, it's home
to a family of white-footed mice.

In all those three years,
the tree hasn't grown at all.
This oak tree is dead.
But—the hole is full of life.

A hairy woodpecker sometimes comes to roost there.

A gray squirrel often uses the hole as a hiding place.

When the hole has water in it, you can sometimes see a tree frog there.

One day lightning, or a high wind,
or heavy rain, or snow
will bring this dead tree down.
Many years later all that may be
left will be a log with a hole in it.

But the hole will still be a place for living things.
A small garter snake may cool off in there.

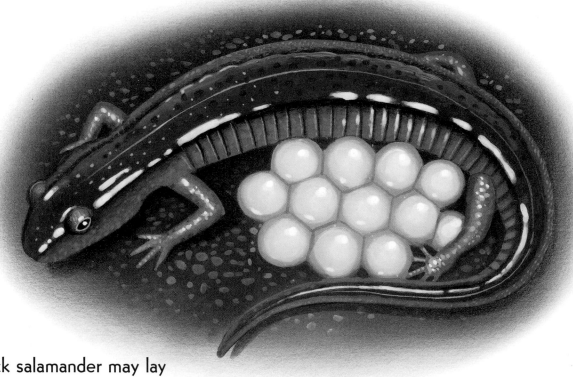

A redback salamander may lay
its eggs there.

Or maybe a hammock spider
will make a web across the hole
to catch swarming insects.

Living trees are important.
But so are dead and dying trees.
A dead tree often has a hole—
one small place that is usually home
for something.